Stories from Faiths

CHRISTIANITY

Susie Hodge

Heinemann
LIBRARY

www.heinemann.co.uk/library
Visit our website to find out more information about Heinemann Library books.

To order:

☎ Phone 44 (0) 1865 888066

🖹 Send a fax to 44 (0) 1865 314091

💻 Visit the Heinemann Bookshop at www.heinemann.co.uk/library to browse our catalogue and order online.

Heinemann Library is an imprint of **Pearson Education Limited**, a company incorporated in England and Wales having its registered office at Edinburgh Gate, Harlow, Essex, CM20 2JE – Registered company number: 00872828

"Heinemann" is a registered trademark of Pearson Education Limited

Editor: Jean Coppendale
Consultant: Council of Christians and Jews (CCJ)
Designers: Harleen Mehta, Neha Gupta
Picture Researcher: Anju Pathak
Art Director: Rahul Dhiman
Client Service Manager: Aparna Malhotra
Project Manager: Smita Mehta
Lineart: Sibi N Devasia
Colouring Artists: Subhash Vohra, Danish Zaidi, Ashish Tanwar
Originated by Chroma Graphics (Overseas) Pte Ltd
Printed and bound in China by CTPS

ISBN 978-0-431-08221-9 (hardback)
13 12 11 10 09
10 9 8 7 6 5 4 3 2 1

British Library Cataloguing in Publication Data

Hodge, Susie
    Christanity. – (Stories from faiths)
    230
A full catalogue record for this book is available from the British Library.

Acknowledgements

We would like to thank the following for permission to reproduce photographs (t = top, b = bottom, c = centre, l = left, r = right, m = middle): G. Campbell/ Shutterstock: 4b, Ginosphotos/ Dreamstime: 5l, Peter N. Lewis: 7tr, Ariel Skelley/ Jupiterimages: 8tl, SW Productions/ Brand X/ Corbis: 11mr, Irina Opachevsky/ Fotolia: 12tl, Jupiterimages: 15tr, lisafx/ Can Stock Photo: 16bl, Digital Planet Design/ iStockphoto: 19tr, U.S. Agency for International Development: 20bl, Raju/ The Hindu: 23tr, Christine Osborne Pictures/ World Religion Photos Picture Library: 25br, Peter Baxter/ Shutterstock: 26tl, Thomas M Perkins/ Shutterstock: 28tl.

Q2A Media Art Bank: 6, 8–9, 10–11, 12–13, 14–15, 16–17, 18–19, 20–21, 22–23, 24–25, 26–27, 28–29.

Cover photograph of a girl sitting in church reading the Bible reproduced with permission of Stockbyte/ Getty Images

We would like to thank **Q2AMEDIA** for invaluable help in the preparation of this book.

Every effort has been made to contact copyright holders of material reproduced in this book. Any omissions will be rectified in subsequent printings if notice is given to the publishers.

Disclaimer

All the Internet addresses (URLs) given in this book were valid at the time of going to press. However, due to the dynamic nature of the Internet, some addresses may have changed, or sites may have changed or ceased to exist since publication. While the author and publishers regret any inconvenience this may cause readers, no responsibility for any such changes can be accepted by either the author or the publishers.

Contents

Some words are printed in bold, **like this**. You can find out what they mean in the glossary.

What is Christianity?

Christianity is a world religion based on the teachings of **Jesus Christ**. The teachings of Jesus are recorded in the New Testament in the Bible. Followers of Christianity are known as Christians. They believe that Jesus was the Son of God who came to Earth about 2,000 years ago to help all people understand God better and to know more about Him.

Christians believe that, when Jesus was about 33 years old, he was tortured and killed by being nailed onto a cross. But they also believe that, most importantly, Jesus then rose from the dead and appeared to his **disciples** (followers). This was to show everyone that there is another life beyond this one, a life with God who will love us forever.

Christians flock to see Pope Benedict XVI in St Peter's Square in Rome. The Pope is the head of the Roman Catholic Church, which is a branch of Christianity.

Christian worship

Christians **worship** God in **churches**, which are often built in the shape of a cross. This is because the Cross is the main **symbol** of Christianity, and it reminds Christians how Jesus died on one to save them. Christian worship involves praising God through music, singing, readings, prayers and special ceremonies and festivals. The most important Christian festivals are Christmas, when Jesus was born, and Easter, when Jesus died and rose again.

A Bible on a lectern, or stand. During a Christian church service, someone usually reads from the Bible.

Holy book

The Bible is the Christian holy book, which is divided into the Old and New Testaments. The Old Testament is the name given by Christians to the ancient Jewish scriptures. Some of the stories are also sacred to Muslims. The New Testament tells of the life and teachings of Jesus and of the first Christians. Jesus often taught by telling stories and **parables**, which are short stories that contain important messages.

The Nativity

One day, a young girl called Mary heard a voice calling her name. She looked up and was amazed to see an **angel** standing there. "You have been chosen to give birth to God's son," the angel told her. Mary felt frightened but she replied, "I am the Lord's servant and I will do whatever He wants."

The Angel Gabriel was sent by God to speak to Mary.

Mary was going to be married to a carpenter called Joseph. When she saw Joseph the next day she told him about the visit from the angel, and that she was going to have a baby. At first he didn't like the idea and told her that he would not marry her after all. Then an angel spoke to Joseph in a dream and told him that God had sent the baby, so Joseph decided to marry Mary and take care of the baby.

Soon after Mary and Joseph were married, the Roman Emperor Augustus sent out an order that there was to be a **census**. This meant that all the people had to go back to the towns where they were born to register their names.

Joseph and Mary packed up a donkey and started out on the long journey to their home town of Bethlehem. The journey was hard, especially for Mary, and there were many people travelling on the roads. "I shall be glad to reach an inn," said Mary to Joseph, "I think the baby will be born soon!"

▲ Children perform a Nativity play which tells the story of the birth of Jesus in the stable at Bethlehem.

Nearly Christmas

Advent is the name given to the four weeks that lead up to Christmas Day. This is the time when Christians prepare to celebrate the birth, or Nativity, of Jesus. Many schools and **churches** put on plays which tell the story of Jesus' birth. They also have special concerts in which everyone sings carols, which are songs that are sung at Christmas time.

▲ Christmas dinner is a traditional meal full of good things to eat, and when family and friends get together.

Big feast

Christmas is an annual holiday on 25 December that celebrates the birth of Jesus. Modern customs include giving presents and cards, church celebrations and putting up special decorations, including Christmas trees, lights, mistletoe, nativity scenes and holly. On Christmas Day, many Christians go to church and then sit down to a meal with family and friends.

Eventually they reached Bethlehem. The town was very crowded and Joseph and Mary had nowhere to stay. Everywhere they went the **innkeepers** told them, "Sorry, no room!"

"Oh, Joseph, what shall we do?" cried Mary. "My baby is nearly due." Then, the last innkeeper they went to took pity on them and called them back.

"I have an idea," the innkeeper said, "you can sleep in my stable! The straw is clean and the animals will keep you warm." Joseph and Mary had no choice, so they settled in the stable for the night. Soon, **Jesus** was born. Mary wrapped him in cloths and laid him in a clean **manger** full of soft straw.

That night, in a nearby field, some shepherds were looking after their sheep. Suddenly, a group of angels appeared and told the shepherds that Jesus, the Son of God, had been born.

Soon after Jesus was born, three wise men came from the East, bringing special gifts for the baby Jesus.

The shepherds gasped in wonder as a great sparkling star appeared in the sky over Bethlehem. The shepherds left their sheep and hurried to the stable, where they saw the tiny baby. "God has sent us His Son!" they whispered joyfully. "We must tell everyone that Jesus is born."

The news about the birth of a special baby soon spread, and three wise men from the East followed the great star in search of the newborn king. When they found the baby Jesus, they gave him special gifts – shining gold, a perfumed oil called **frankincense** and sweet-smelling **myrrh**.

The Lost Sheep

Wherever **Jesus** went, large crowds followed him to hear his stories and **parables**. One day, among the people who crowded around him were some Pharisees, who made sure that people obeyed the Jewish law, as well as poor people and even thieves. Jesus told them all this story:

There was once a shepherd who looked after 100 sheep. He loved the sheep and knew each one by name. The sheep recognised the shepherd's voice and trusted him to look after them. Every day, the sheep followed him because he always found them the best places with the juiciest grass. The shepherd stayed with his sheep all day and protected them from any attackers, even though it was often dangerous for him. "I am just like the good shepherd," Jesus explained. "The people who follow me trust me and I look after them."

The good shepherd took great care of all of his sheep.

One evening,
the shepherd
was counting his
sheep into the **fold**,
as he did at the end of each
day, "One, two, three … 97, 98, 99
…Oh no! There's one missing!"

The shepherd looked and looked,
but it was definitely not amongst his
flock. What could have happened
to it? Had it been stolen? Had it
wandered away and been eaten by a
lion, or fallen off a cliff? Worried and
sad, the shepherd left his other 99
sheep safely in their fold and went
off to search for the lost one.

God cares

Jesus taught that God cares
for everyone in the same way
that a shepherd cares for
his sheep. Christians also
believe that poor and
needy people should be
treated with kindness
and helped as much
as possible.

▼ These young people are
giving food and water to
help homeless people.

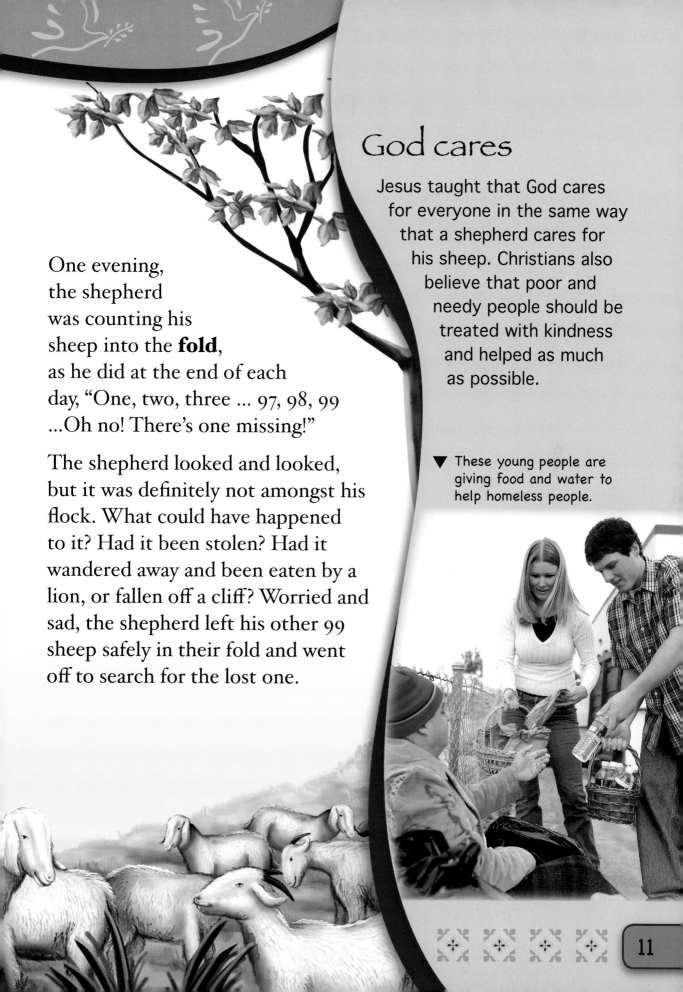

11

At last, he found the lost, frightened sheep, high up on a mountain crag. The shepherd was delighted.

"Don't worry," he called to the sheep, "I will rescue you!" He climbed the crag and carefully lifted the sheep on to his strong shoulders. Picking his way carefully over the rocky ground, he carried it safely back to the rest of the flock.

Then the shepherd called his friends together: "Come and celebrate with me!" he cried joyfully. "I'm so happy that I've found my lost sheep that I'm going to throw a party!"

▲ A shepherd working in the **Middle East** today, looking after his sheep in the same way that shepherds did 2,000 years ago.

Good shepherds

Keeping sheep is still common in the **Middle East** today. The sheep are valuable for their wool, milk and meat. The way in which shepherds keep and care for their sheep is almost the same as it was 2,000 years ago.

The story that Jesus told about the lost sheep had an additional meaning, which he wanted the people to understand. Those people who turn their backs on God and forget Him are just like the lost sheep. But, like the good shepherd, God will always search for one "lost" person and help to make that person feel loved and safe – even though there are many other people who remain faithful to Him. Everyone matters to God.

The shepherd found his lost sheep frightened and alone on a high mountain crag,

The Good Samaritan

One day, a man asked **Jesus** a difficult question. "What must I do on Earth to make sure that I go to Heaven when I die?" he asked. Jesus replied, "What does God's law tell us about that?"

The man answered, "That we must love God with all our hearts, and love our neighbours, just as we love ourselves."

"Yes," Jesus nodded. "That's right." But the man was not satisfied.

A man was travelling along a lonely road, when he was attacked by thieves.

"So who exactly are "my neighbours"?" he asked. Jesus told a story to explain.

One day, a Jew was walking from Jerusalem to Jericho. Nobody liked using this lonely road as there were lots of large rocks where robbers could hide. Suddenly, a group of bandits jumped out from behind the rocks. They snatched the man's bag, stole his donkey and his cloak and beat him up. Then they ran off, leaving him to die.

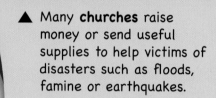

▲ Many **churches** raise money or send useful supplies to help victims of disasters such as floods, famine or earthquakes.

Giving

Christians try to behave as Jesus taught them to. They believe we should all treat each other with kindness. Many Christians collect money to give to charities, or they give their belongings to charity shops to be sold or sent to the needy. A good Christian always thinks of others and tries to help whenever possible.

Caring

Christians believe that we must all care for and help each other. In the story of the Good Samaritan, Jesus was making the point that everyone is our neighbour and should receive our love, compassion and help.

▼ Christians believe that they should help others whenever they can.

After a while, a priest passed by. He noticed the badly injured man, but didn't stop and hurried on his way. Shortly after, another man came along the road. He was a Levi, a well-known teacher in the **synagogue**. But he was also sped past the wounded man on the other side of the road.

Some time later, a **Samaritan**, travelling on a donkey, saw the man. Now Jews and Samaritans hated each other, but the Samaritan felt sorry for the man who was lying in the hot sun, badly wounded. The Samaritan cleaned the man's wounds, then he bandaged him and lifted him on to his donkey and led him to the nearest inn. When he arrived, the Samaritan gave the **innkeeper** some money. "Please take care of this man," he said. "When I come back this way, if you have spent more money to look after him, I will repay you whatever it costs."

When he had told his story, Jesus looked at the man and said, "Which of the three passers by showed love to the injured man?"

"The one who looked after him," answered the man, who didn't like admitting it was the Samaritan. Jesus replied, "That's right. Everyone is your neighbour. Now you go and behave in the same way."

The Samaritan bathed the man's wounds and looked after him.

Feeding the Five Thousand

As well as telling stories, **Jesus** also performed **miracles**. He became known for his power to heal the sick, help the blind to see and the lame to walk. Jesus became so popular that he was followed by crowds of people wherever he went.

One day, Jesus and his **disciples** sailed across the Sea of Galilee to a peaceful place for a rest. But the people found out where he was going and thousands followed him there.

Jesus held up the bread and fish and blessed it. How could five small loaves and two small fish feed so many thousands of people?

The disciples wanted to send the people away. But when Jesus saw how much they needed him, he walked amongst them, helping them and talking to them. By the evening, his disciples said, "Jesus, surely it's time you sent everyone away? You're tired and everyone is hungry – they need to go and find some food."

"There is no need for them to go," said Jesus. "You can give everyone a meal."

"But there must be at least five thousand people here!" the disciples exclaimed. "We don't have nearly enough money to buy food for everyone."

Andrew, one of the disciples, spoke. "A boy over there has offered his lunch to Jesus. But he only has five loaves of bread and two small fish. That won't go far in this crowd!"

▲ A family says grace and thanks God for their food before they eat their meal.

Saying grace

Many Christians say a short prayer before they eat a meal, thanking God for the food they are about to eat. This is called "saying grace". This helps Christians to remember the good things they have, such as food and friendship, and that there are people who are not as fortunate as they are, and who do not have much food.

Christian Aid

Christian Aid is an organisation that helps poor and distressed people around the world. Christians give money which pays for food and other things people need. Christian Aid workers give out food to poor people, remembering the way in which Jesus fed the poor and hungry in the Bible.

▼ This hungry child is receiving hot, nourishing soup from a Christian Aid worker.

Then Jesus told all the people to sit down. The boy gave Jesus his small basket of food. "Thank you," said Jesus, smiling.

Then Jesus prayed and thanked God for the food they had been given. He broke the loaves into small pieces and divided the fish. Then he turned to his disciples and said, "Give some of this food to everyone here."

Suddenly the basket was overflowing with fresh fish and sweet-smelling bread. The people gasped for there was more than enough food for everyone there.

Even when all the people had eaten and gone home, Jesus told his disciples, "Gather up all the pieces of bread and fish that are left. Let nothing be wasted."

The disciples filled twelve baskets with the food that was left over.

Jesus' disciples gave out the food to the hungry people. There was more than enough to go round.

Jairus' Daughter

Jesus was walking through the streets when a man named Jairus, the leader of a Jewish **synagogue**, pushed his way through the crowd. "Jesus! Please come quickly!" he begged, pulling at Jesus' sleeve. "My young daughter is dying." Jesus saw that Jairus had great faith in him, so he went with Jairus to see the sick child.

On the way, a servant from Jairus' house rushed up to them. "Your daughter has died," the servant said quickly. Poor Jairus! He thought his heart would break. Jesus turned to him. "Don't be afraid. Trust me, Jairus, and all will be well."

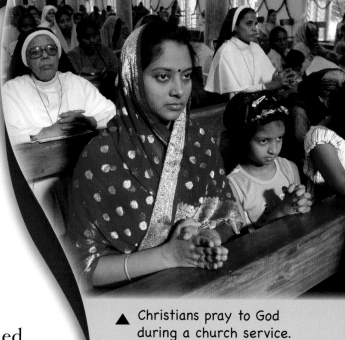

At Jairus' house, people were weeping over the girl's death. "What's all this noise for?" asked Jesus. "She's only sleeping." Then Jesus went into the girl's room.

He took the girl's hand gently in his. "Get up, little one," Jesus said softly. At once, the girl opened her eyes, smiled at him and stood up. Her parents hugged her and wept with joy. Jesus had given them back their much-loved daughter.

▲ Christians pray to God during a church service.

Jesus brought Jairus' daughter back to life.

The power of prayer

Jesus taught that we should always be kind and **compassionate** towards each other, and if anyone asks for our help, we should do what we can for them. Christians also believe in the power of prayer. Many Christians pray to God together during **church** services.

The Easter Story

The Jewish priests in Jerusalem were jealous of **Jesus** and his popularity. They had a meeting, and decided on a plan to have him arrested and killed. When the priests asked him, "Are you the Son of God?", he replied, "I am." They decided that Jesus was guilty of claiming to be equal with God, so they took him to the Roman ruler, Pontius Pilate.

Jesus was bound as a prisoner and taken before the Roman ruler, Pontius Pilate.

"We've brought you a trouble maker, Pilate," the priests explained. "This man has been going around telling people not to pay their taxes and even calls himself a king!"

Pilate looked at Jesus, "Are you a king?" he asked.

"So you say," Jesus replied, but he would not answer any more questions.

Pilate knew that Jesus did not deserve to die, but the priests wanted him killed. It was the time of the **Passover** festival and there was a tradition that each year, one prisoner chosen by the people was released. Pilate asked the crowd who had gathered, "Which prisoner do you wish me to set free, the murderer Barabbas, or Jesus Christ?"

The crowd, led by the jealous priests, called out, "Free Barabbas!"

So then Pilate asked, "Then what shall I do with Jesus?"

"Crucify him!" yelled the crowd.

"Why, what crime has he done?" asked Pilate. But the crowd just shouted louder, "Crucify him!"

Holy Week

Easter is the most important of all the Christian festivals. The week leading up to Easter is called Holy Week, when Christians remember the Easter story and many **churches** hold special services every day. In churches, people read in the Bible about the last few days of Jesus' life.

▼ This priest is carrying a large wooden cross through the streets during Holy Week.

▲ Many people eat hot cross buns on Good Friday.

Hot cross buns

On Good Friday (the name is thought to have started as "God's Friday") Christians remember how Jesus died on the cross, and many go to special church services. It is traditional to eat hot cross buns on Good Friday. These are warmed, sweet buns decorated with white pastry crosses, that **symbolise** the crucifixion.

Then the Roman soldiers took Jesus away, and whipped him and tore his clothes.

"You call yourself King of the Jews? Here, have this crown of thorns!" they laughed. They had made Jesus a crown out of thorns and squashed it on his head. Then they jeered and called out to him, "Hail, King of the Jews!"

The day of Jesus' **crucifixion** came, and the soldiers forced him to drag a heavy wooden cross through the streets of Jerusalem. Jesus was to be crucified outside the city gates at the top of a hill called Golgotha, which means "the place of the skull". A large crowd followed, mocking Jesus as he stumbled and struggled under the weight of the cross.

At Golgotha, Jesus was nailed to the cross, which was raised up and fixed in the ground. Two robbers were put on crosses on either side of him.

"Aren't you the Christ? Why don't you save yourself and us?" called out one robber.

But the other robber said, "We're getting what we deserve. But this man has done nothing wrong. Remember me when you reach your kingdom," he said to Jesus.

"Today you will be with me in paradise," Jesus comforted him.

At noon, when the sun should have been at its brightest, the sky went black. For three hours, it stayed dark while Jesus suffered. His friends, some of his **disciples** and his mother wept at the foot of the cross.

Then suddenly, Jesus lifted his head to the sky and called out, "My God, why have you left me?" Soon after, Jesus bowed his head and died.

Jesus was made to carry his cross through the streets of Jerusalem. The people and the Roman soldiers laughed and jeered as he passed by.

Children often decorate eggs with patterns and colours ready for Easter Day celebrations.

New life

Easter is the festival when Christians remember how Jesus died and then rose from the dead. Many Christians celebrate by going to church. It is traditional to give and receive Easter eggs. The eggs symbolise new life and hope for the future. Easter is a time of new life, when baby animals are born and the first spring flowers appear.

Joseph of Arimathea was one of Jesus' followers. He went to Pilate and begged for Jesus' body. Helped by another man, Nicodemus, he wrapped Jesus' body in a linen sheet and took it to a garden nearby where a tomb had been cut into a rock.

Two friends of Jesus, Mary Magdalene and another Mary, followed. They watched while the men rolled a heavy stone in front of the entrance to the tomb and then, grief-stricken, they all went home.

Jesus had died on Friday afternoon and the next day was the Sabbath, the Jewish day of rest. The hours passed slowly for Jesus' heartbroken friends.

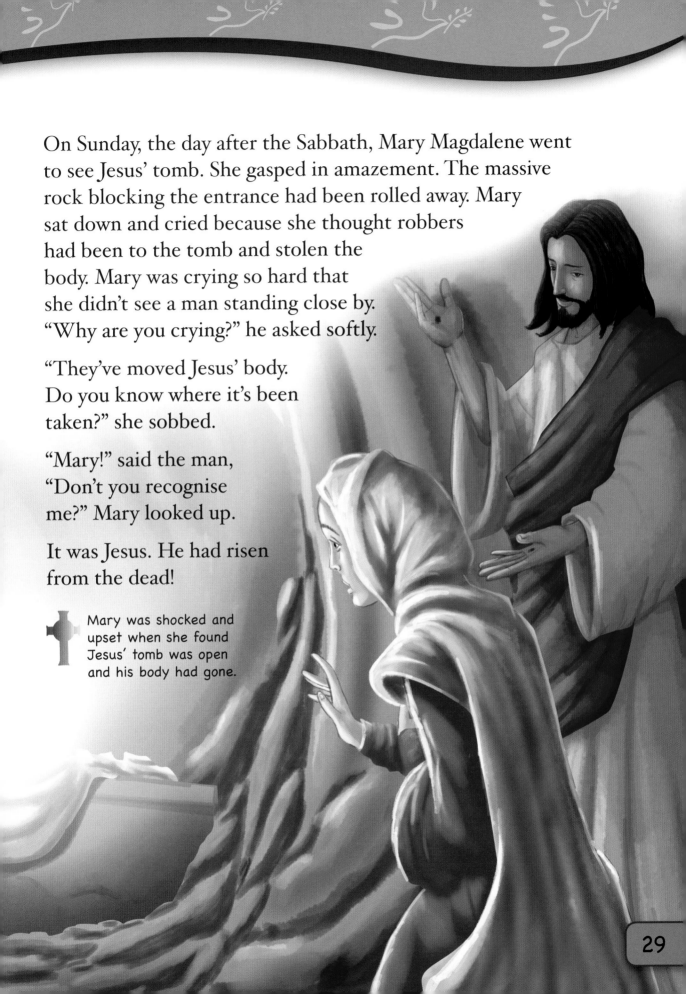

On Sunday, the day after the Sabbath, Mary Magdalene went to see Jesus' tomb. She gasped in amazement. The massive rock blocking the entrance had been rolled away. Mary sat down and cried because she thought robbers had been to the tomb and stolen the body. Mary was crying so hard that she didn't see a man standing close by. "Why are you crying?" he asked softly.

"They've moved Jesus' body. Do you know where it's been taken?" she sobbed.

"Mary!" said the man, "Don't you recognise me?" Mary looked up.

It was Jesus. He had risen from the dead!

Mary was shocked and upset when she found Jesus' tomb was open and his body had gone.

Glossary

angel – heavenly beings or messengers of God

census – official count of people in a country

church – building used for worship by most Christians. The word *Church* with a capital "C" also means a group of Christians.

compassion – kindness and concern for others

crucifixion – how Jesus was killed: nailed to a wooden cross

disciple – the twelve men Jesus chose to be his closest followers

fold (for sheep) – small building where sheep are kept at night

frankincense – a sweet-smelling oil used to perfume homes

innkeeper – someone in charge of an inn, or small hotel

Jesus (also called **Jesus Christ**) – a Jewish teacher. Christians believe Jesus was the Son of God. *Christ* means "chosen by God"

manger – open feeding box for an animal

miracle – wondrous event that cannot be explained

Middle East – the countries of Southwest Asia and North Africa – usually including countries from Libya in the West and Iran in the East.

myrrh – a scented substance that is used as incense, in perfume or medicine

parable – a simple story with an important message

Passover – a festival when Jews remember how they were saved from slavery in Egypt in ancient times

Pharisee – man who was a member of a group of strict followers of Jewish law

Samaritan – someone from the area called Samaria

symbol – an object or sign that stands for, or represents, something else

synagogue – Jewish place of worship

tomb – burial place, usually made of stone

worship – take part in a religious service

Find out more

Websites

atschool.eduweb.co.uk/carolrb/christianity/
Finding out about Christianity around the world.

www.firstschoolyears.com/re/christianity/christianity.htm
Information and pictures about Jesus' life and teachings, plus
Christian beliefs, celebrations and festivals.

www.jesusandkidz.com/
Stories, songs and activities about Christianity.

Books

Christianity (Eyewitness) by Philip Wilkinson
Publisher: Dorling Kindersley, 2006

Stories Jesus Told: Favourite Stories from the Bible, Nick Butterworth
and Nick Inkpen
Publisher: Candle Books, 2005

The Lion Encyclopaedia of Christianity by David Self
Publisher: Lion Hudson, 2007

This Is My Faith: Christianity by Holly Wallace
Publisher: Barron's Educational Series, 2006

Index